Contents

Who Were the Tudors?

The Tudor age began in 1485, when Henry Tudor was crowned King Henry VII of England at the end of the Wars of the Roses. It lasted until the death of Queen Elizabeth I, in 1603.

In 1509, Henry VII was succeeded by his son, King Henry VIII. The young king was popular with his people. He built fine palaces, and fought wars against France and Scotland. But in time, Henry brought religious upheaval to England. When he became king, most people belonged to the Catholic Church, which was headed by the Pope, in Rome. In 1534, Henry broke away from the Catholic Church and proclaimed himself head of the Church of England. The land and riches of the Church became Henry's property and he sold off most of this land to dukes, barons and other noblemen.

The noblemen made money from their land by farming sheep and charging high rents. They could afford the best things in life and they had plenty of leisure time to enjoy them. Games of cards, and board games such as chess and backgammon were popular pastimes. Books were rare, so only the rich could afford them.

(Right) A wealthy baron and his family, wearing clothes typical of the rich in Tudor times, spend the afternoon playing games and drinking wine in their manor house.

Baron   Playing cards   Backgammon   Leather boots   Wine

Head-dress   Feather cap   Hose (trousers)   Sheepskin rug   Sheath of daggers

THE TUDORS
RECONSTRUCTED

Liz Gogerly
Photographs by Martyn F. Chillmaid

HODDER
Wayland
An imprint of Hodder Children's Books

RECONSTRUCTED

Other titles in this series:
The Home Front • The Romans
The Saxons and Vikings • The Victorians

For more information on this series and other Hodder Wayland titles, go to www.hodderwayland.co.uk

Conceived and produced for Hodder Wayland by

Nutshell
MEDIA

Intergen House, 65–67 Western Road, Hove BN3 2JQ, UK
www.nutshellmedialtd.co.uk

Editor: Polly Goodman
Designer: Simon Borrough
All reconstructions set-up and photographed by: Martyn F. Chillmaid

First published in Great Britain in 2003 by Hodder Wayland,
an imprint of Hodder Children's Books.

This paperback edition published in 2005

Gogerly, Liz
The Tudors. – (Reconstructed)
1. Great Britain – Social life and customs – 16th century – Pictorial works – Juvenile literature
2. Great Britain – History – Tudors, 1485-1603 – Pictorial works – Juvenile literature
I. Title
942'.05'0222

ISBN 0 7502 4768 1

Printed and bound in China

Hodder Children's Books
A division of Hodder Headline Limited
338 Euston Road, London NW1 3BH

Cover photographs: main photo: A baron's family relax in their manor house; from top to bottom: a schoolboy and his tutor; infantrymen defending their house from a castle battlements; a Catholic family attend a secret mass in their house; a cook prepares a feast in a manor house kitchen; a peasant woman carries a bucket of water from the nearest well.

Title page: A baron's family celebrate some good news with a banquet.

Riches for the Rich

Wealthy Tudors loved to show off their riches. The clothes people wore and the homes they lived in were all signs of their place in society. Nobles had magnificent manor houses built and wore elaborate clothing made from the best cloth available. Food was another show of wealth. The rich could afford all kinds of meats and fish, and expensive French wine. Holidays were celebrated with lavish banquets, usually accompanied by music and dancing. At the court of King Henry VIII, it wasn't unusual for ten courses to be served over seven hours.

Other European nations believed the English had barbarian tastes in food. During Henry's reign, people feasted on robins, seagulls, badgers, tortoises and otters. The best food was considered to be roast veal and venison. Sugar was another delicacy because it had to be imported from the Americas, so it was expensive. In 1541, a law was passed to stop people eating too much. Nobles were allowed a maximum of seven main dishes at a meal, gentlemen were allowed five and everyone else was allowed four.

Jug of wine

Silver cup

Musician

Wooden bowls

Waiting staff

Serving boy

A baron's family celebrates some good news with a banquet.

The type of sports or pastime a person did was another sign of their rank or wealth. The rich had time for falconry, hunting, jousting, tennis and bowls. Falconry was popular with the Tudor kings as well as the aristocracy and lesser noblemen. Falcons or other birds of prey were trained to hunt birds or small mammals and bring them back to their keeper. Again, the type of bird a person kept was an indication of their position in society. King Henry VIII had one of the largest falcons, a gyr, which gave spectacular displays at the royal court. The birds of lesser noblemen were smaller and were used for hunting game. Falconry was taken so seriously by the Tudors that poaching falcon chicks or eggs by night in private forests was an offence punishable by death.

A falconer prepares to let his bird fly and hunt for game.

Leather glove

Buzzard

Dagger handle

Slashing (clothes style)

Rags for the Poor

While the rich had time for leisure, the poor worked hard and struggled to survive. They were expected to work all the hours of daylight for six days a week. Public holidays, or holy days, were often the only time they could have fun.

Peasant meals were based around coarse grey bread made from rye or barley. Soups were made from the vegetables and herbs that grew nearby. Meat was a luxury, but peasants sometimes kept animals to provide milk, cheese and eggs. Water from the nearest well or river was often so dirty that people brewed their own ale or beer to drink instead.

Life for the poor in Tudor times was harsh, but most people accepted their place in society. They believed that it was God's will that some people were superior to others, and that there was a 'Great Chain', with God at the top. Below God came the King, then clergymen and nobles. In the middle there were gentlemen, such as rich merchants or landowners. At the bottom were peasants, followed by animals. People accepted God's will on Earth to ensure their place in Heaven.

A peasant woman struggles with her buckets of water, collected from the nearest well.

Bucket of water

Yoke

Woollen dress

					A boy aims a handful of dung at the vagabond in the pillory.
Pillory	Guard	Market stall	Dung	Spectator	

When the harvest failed it was tempting for poor people to steal food. In villages, people tended to band together and help each other during difficult times. When people did break the law, they risked public flogging or being hanged. Vagabonds were travelling people who refused to work. They drifted from village to village, begging and stealing. If they were caught cheating, they might be placed in the pillory for a few days, where villagers threw rotten food and dung at them. Sometimes criminals had their ears nailed to the pillory, too.

Hygiene and Disease

In the heat of the summer, the smell in the towns became unbearable. Part of the problem was the growth of the towns, to which a steady stream of people had migrated from the countryside in search of work. They lived in ramshackle houses with no proper drainage. Open sewers often ran down the middle of the streets. Homes for the rich were better, but their toilets were built on the sides of their houses so the human waste fell into pits outside. Nobody could escape the appalling filth, but nosegays (sweet-smelling flowers and herbs) helped when the stench became too much.

Washer women do the laundry of a rich family in a river. They used a type of soap made from wood ash, water and animal fat or oil. They also used urine to wash their laundry, rubbing and beating the clothes against rocks to remove the dirt. Later, the clothes were hung out to dry on bushes.

In Tudor times, nobody realized that diseases were caused by lack of hygiene and overcrowding. The open sewers flowed directly into rivers and wells, from where people collected drinking water. Diseases like cholera, which is passed through human faeces, were common. Townhouses were built close together and families often slept with more than one in a bed. This allowed infectious diseases such as smallpox to spread quickly because they are passed through people's breath. The only way the Tudors knew to prevent the spread of disease was to separate the healthy from the sick. When the plague broke out in London in 1563, the court of Elizabeth I escaped to Windsor for the summer.

A servant empties the slops out of a window into the street below.

Slops

Timber-framed house

Latticed windows

Supporting beams

Making a Living

Although towns were beginning to grow in Tudor times, most people still lived and worked in the countryside. Shepherding was a traditional job at the heart of England's wool trade. The only tools a shepherd required were a crook to catch the sheep, a pair of shears and a tar box. He used tar to treat the wounds of injured sheep and to mark them for their owner.

Many landowners grew rich on the wool trade. Wool and woven cloth were exported throughout Europe, and to the new colonies in America and the East and West Indies. The Cotswolds, East Anglia and Yorkshire became centres of the cloth trade. There was plenty of work for craftsmen such as spinners, weavers, dyers and tailors. Each group of craftsmen formed an organization called a guild, which had its own set of rules to maintain the quality of their work. The guild took on apprentices to make sure that members were properly trained, and provided support for the families of members who were ill.

A shepherd watches over a flock of sheep for the farmer.

Crook

Woollen cap

Woollen tunic

Woollen hose

Wealth from the wool trade meant that noblemen, landowners and merchants could afford to build grand houses or palaces made of stone instead of wood. To build their dream homes they employed the skill of a stone mason. The mason had the role of builder, architect and engineer all in one. He carved blocks of stone on the floor before putting them in place.

To make sure he was paid for his work, each mason carved his own mark into the stone. If you look closely at Tudor stonework today you can still see these marks. The Tudors also built magnificent castles. Masons had to work at great heights and were often injured or killed in falls. They formed one of the most powerful guilds to look after its members in case of accidents.

Chisel   Hammer

Block of stone   Mallet

A stone mason carefully carves a block of stone using tools that have not changed for centuries.

Women's Work

In a world without machinery, where nearly everything had to be done by hand, poor women had to work hard. They were responsible for running the home and looking after children. Tidiness was considered a virtue, so they rose early in the morning to start their chores. As well as cooking, washing and cleaning, women made soap, candles and clothes. They had wool to spin and honey to collect. In the countryside, they helped to grow vegetables and look after the livestock. Women also took paid work. In the towns they were cooks, servants, weavers, milliners, shopkeepers, wetnurses and barmaids.

Pig on spit   Basket of apples   Wooden barrels

Lantern   Sack of unspun wool   Spindle

A cook and her daughter prepare a feast in the kitchen of a manor house.

A gentlewoman checks the quality of some cheese before she buys it from a market stall.

In Tudor times it would never do for a husband to be caught shopping for food – that was, most certainly, the job of his wife! In the countryside, most shopping took place in the local marketplace. People took their own produce to sell and would buy from other local people. Eggs, cheese, vegetables and meat were usually on offer.

Though men were the main breadwinners, some women ran their own businesses. They had shops, inns and ale-houses, or went on the road selling lace, haberdashery and other goods. Some craftswomen became so successful they banded together to form their own guilds. Despite their success, women were never considered to be equal with men. They were called the weaker sex and were believed to be less reliable than men. All women were expected to marry young, bear children and obey their husbands.

Gentlewoman   Stallholder

Apples   Cheese

Bread   Eggs and vegetables

A Tudor Childhood

Education in Tudor times was mainly for boys, from families who could afford to pay for it. Boys began school at the age of 4 and moved to a grammar school when they were 7. At the beginning of the sixteenth century most schools were part of the Church and boys were taught Latin so they could study the Bible. School days were long, starting at 6 a.m. and finishing at 5.30 p.m. to make the most of the daylight. Schoolchildren had Thursdays and Sundays off, and holidays at Christmas and Easter.

There were few books, so pupils read from hornbooks instead. These wooden boards had the alphabet, prayers or other writing pinned to them and were covered with a thin layer of transparent cow's horn. The teachers were strict. Laughing, pulling faces or even yawning was not tolerated and pupils were often whipped.

Only girls from wealthy backgrounds received any education, and this was usually at home. The most important thing was that they were groomed to find rich husbands.

Hornbook

Latin book

Woollen doublet

Woollen breeches

Under the watchful eye of his teacher, a schoolboy reads from his hornbook.

The son of a merchant shows off his string-driven mill to his friends.

While the boys from noble or rich families went to school, poorer children started work. By the time they were 6 or 7, most children were working or helping at home. If they were lucky, boys learned a trade and took a seven-year apprenticeship.

Long hours studying or working didn't stop Tudor children playing games and having fun. Toys were often made from wood or materials that were easily available, such as stone, clay or animal bones. They were made by children's parents, or children made their own toys from things people didn't want. Pig's bladders were blown up to make footballs, hoops were made from old barrels, and pebbles or cherry stones were used to play marbles or jacks. Children also played games like blind man's buff and leapfrog, or 'let's pretend' games like 'shopkeepers'.

A selection of popular Tudor toys.

Spinning tops

Bear on a stick

Wooden jack stones

Windmill

Clay marbles

Bartholomew Babies (dolls)

All the King's Soldiers

In 1485, Henry VII had toppled Richard III from the throne to become king. Throughout his reign, he was afraid that somebody would attempt to do the same to him. In fact, Henry VII brought peace and stability to England.

His son Henry VIII, however, wanted to bring glory to his country by fighting France, conquering Wales and keeping the Scottish at bay. In the 1530s, King Henry VIII began building a string of castles and gun forts along England's south coast. He also ordered the expansion of the navy. In the summer of 1545, when Francis I of France threatened to invade England, Henry was ready to show off his military might. In the Battle of Portsmouth that followed, the French retreated but Henry's great battleship, the *Mary Rose*, sank.

Infantrymen practise using their weapons from a castle.

Matchlock (gun)   Match

Plate armour   Sword handle

Longbow and arrow   Italian bill

Further attempts by the French to invade England in the summer of 1545 were also unsuccessful, although they did capture the Isle of Wight. On 25 July, French troops landed at Seaford, in Sussex, but English soldiers captured and killed the French commander and some of his men. When the rest of the French forces retreated back to France, Henry VIII was victorious.

Henry VIII's daughter Queen Elizabeth I hated war, but in 1588, England was threatened by invasion. King Phillip II of Spain attempted to remove Elizabeth from the throne by sending a massive fleet of ships known as the Armada to England. When the English navy defeated the Armada, Elizabeth captured the love and respect of her people.

Yew bow

Hemp string

Quiver of arrows

Hunting dog

At the beginning of the Tudor period, England relied on the skill of its archers in war. But by 1590 the longbow had been replaced by muskets and guns, and archery became a popular sport instead.

Religious Tension

In 1534, King Henry VIII announced that he was head of the Church of England, instead of the Pope. Henry wanted to divorce his first wife and marry his new love, Anne Boleyn, but the Pope refused to give him permission. Making himself head of the Church was Henry's solution.

As Supreme Head of the Church of England, Henry sold land that had belonged to the Church and many monasteries were destroyed or turned into private homes. In 1539, Archbishop Thomas Cranmer persuaded the King to translate the Bible and the Prayer Book from Latin into English. Laws were passed so that only the official English Bible could be read in church. Catholics who wished to read from the Latin Bible had to do so in secret, and people who refused to attend Church of England ceremonies on Sundays or holy days were fined.

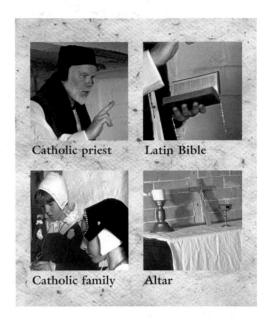

Catholic priest Latin Bible

Catholic family Altar

A Catholic family attend a secret Mass in their house.

Priest

Soldier

Dagger

In a surprise search of a Catholic house, a priest is discovered hiding in a priest hole.

Henry's break with the Catholic Church set in motion years of religious turmoil. His daughter Mary was Catholic. When she became queen, in 1553, she attempted to reverse her father's changes. She had hundreds of Protestants put to death and married the Catholic King Philip of Spain. Her half-sister Elizabeth, who became queen in 1558, was Protestant. She tried to control the religious situation by steering a 'middle way', but Catholic plots against her life meant that more laws were passed against Catholics.

During the reign of Elizabeth I, Catholic priests risked their lives performing private ceremonies in people's houses. Many new homes were built with secret passages and rooms called priest holes, where priests could hide if the house was searched. If discovered, the penalty could be death by being hung, drawn and quartered.

Explorers

In Tudor times, life at sea was risky and dangerous, but it also offered adventure, fame and riches. In November 1577, Sir Francis Drake (1540–96) began his most famous round-the-world voyage on his ship, the *Golden Hind*. When he returned, nearly three years later, Drake was laden with gold and treasures plundered from Spanish ships and from South American settlements. The Spanish accused him of piracy, but he earned the respect of Queen Elizabeth I, probably because she took a share of the fortune.

Drake became a national hero and was knighted by the queen in 1580. In 1588 he served Elizabeth I once more when he fought against the Spanish Armada. In 1596, he died of dysentery on an expedition to the West Indies.

Sir Humphrey Gilbert (1539–83) was the stepbrother of another great explorer and favourite of Elizabeth I, Sir Walter Raleigh. Like his stepbrother, Gilbert dreamed of exploring new lands and in June 1583 he set off to America to found a new colony. Gilbert sailed from Plymouth with five ships, including the *Golden Hind*. In July he landed at St Johns in Newfoundland and set up the first English colony in North America. After two weeks, Gilbert boarded his ship the *Squirrel* to explore the area. On 9 September, the ship was sunk near the Azore Islands and Gilbert was drowned.

(Right) A scouting party comes ashore at Newfoundland, in modern-day Canada.

Officer in charge   Pistol   Italian bill   Pikeman and pike

Standard   Archer   Sword   Halberd

Entertainment

Music played an important part in the daily lives of the Tudors. Nobles and rich families employed travelling musicians who entertained them in their homes, and singing and composing songs were popular pastimes. Henry VIII played the lute and composed his own music. It is rumoured that he wrote the love song 'Greensleeves'.

Elizabeth I enjoyed playing musical instruments too, especially the virginal, which was an early kind of keyboard. Her court was also famous for its dancing. The queen never married, but dancing was a way for her to flirt and enjoy the company of men.

Many of the instruments played by the Tudors are similar to those we use today. The *viola da braccio* (which translated from Italian means 'arm fiddle') was an early violin, and the small harp has developed into the large orchestral harp. Some instruments, such as the hurdy-gurdy, are unfamiliar. The hurdy-gurdy was played by turning the handle and pressing the keys at the same time.

Musicians employed by a nobleman strike up a ballad for his guests.

Viola da braccio

Lute

Cittern

Hurdy-gurdy

Harp

Bagpipe

Peasants had little time for entertainment, but during their holidays and religious festivals they enjoyed singing, dancing, drinking and eating, as well as playing games and watching plays. Morris dancing was usually performed by a troupe of men dressed in white. Sometimes they wore ribbons or bells, and carried sticks and handkerchiefs. A musician played a hurdy-gurdy while the men performed a fertility dance to celebrate death and rebirth. They would travel from village to village, performing in market squares and inn yards.

There were travelling actors who performed their plays in the open air, too. During Elizabeth I's reign, the Swan and the Globe theatres were built beside the River Thames, in London. The queen often came to see the plays of William Shakespeare. *The Merry Wives of Windsor* was one of her favourites.

Bells   Ribbons

Woollen shirt   Woollen waistcoat

Hurdy-gurdy   Spectator

Morris dancers perform a fertility dance in the village square.

In the Tavern

During the reign of Elizabeth I, when England's towns began to grow, many taverns and ale houses were opened. Ale houses were rough places that sold only beer or ale. Taverns were more comfortable venues, which served wine and food. They attracted a better class of customer, such as bankers, lawyers and playwrights. Even so, taverns were often rowdy and filled with drunken, brawling people.

As well as enjoying music and song, customers could play games like draughts, cards or dice, and eat a good cheap meal. The Tudors had a hearty appetite for blood sports and violence. A trip to an ale house could be combined with gambling on a cockerel fight or badger-baiting. Bear-baiting was a particularly cruel form of entertainment. It involved chaining a bear to a post and watching as the bear tried to fend off fierce dogs that leapt up to tear out its throat.

As taverns became more popular, they started to attract thieves and prostitutes. A strict religious group called the Puritans, who were against drinking and gambling, thought taverns were places of sin, and tried to have them closed down.

Most taverns had a painted sign hanging outside, perhaps a picture of a spotted dog, a black lion or a white swan. Many pubs are still known by the names they were given in Tudor times.

(Right) Customers at the tavern enjoy a plate of pig's trotters and a game of draughts.

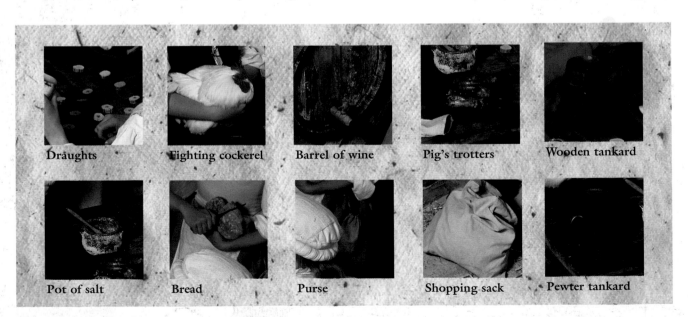

Draughts   Fighting cockerel   Barrel of wine   Pig's trotters   Wooden tankard

Pot of salt   Bread   Purse   Shopping sack   Pewter tankard

Timeline

1485 Henry Tudor defeats Richard III at the Battle of Bosworth and becomes King Henry VII of England, the first of the Tudor monarchs.

1509 Henry VII dies. His son becomes King Henry VIII and marries Catherine of Aragon.

1513 Henry VIII invades France and King James IV of Scotland is killed at the Battle of Flodden.

1516 Catherine of Aragon gives birth to Mary, who later becomes Queen Mary I.

1528 Henry VIII sacks Cardinal Wolsey for failing to persuade the Pope to grant him a divorce.

1533 Henry VIII divorces Catherine of Aragon and marries Anne Boleyn. Anne gives birth to Elizabeth, who later becomes Queen Elizabeth I.

1534 Henry VIII proclaims himself the Supreme Head of the Church of England.

1536 Henry VIII begins closing down the monasteries. Anne Boleyn is executed and Henry marries Jane Seymour.

1537 Jane Seymour gives birth to Edward, who later becomes King Edward VI. Jane Seymour dies.

1539 Publication of the English translation of the Bible.

1538 Henry VIII is excommunicated by the Pope.

1540 Henry VIII marries Anne of Cleves, then divorces her and marries Catherine Howard.

1542 Catherine Howard is executed, and Henry VIII marries Catherine Parr.

1544 Henry VIII invades northern France.

1545 The French attempt to invade England and the *Mary Rose* sinks near Portsmouth.

1547 Henry VIII dies and 9-year old Edward VI becomes king.

1553 Edward VI dies and is succeeded by his half-sister, Mary I. Mary makes England a Roman Catholic country again.

1554 Mary I marries Philip, son of King Charles V of Spain.

1558 Mary I dies and is succeeded by her half-sister Queen Elizabeth I.

1559 Elizabeth I begins reversing the changes that Mary I has made and England becomes a Protestant country again.

1568 Elizabeth I has Mary Queen of Scots imprisoned.

1570 Elizabeth I is excommunicated by the Pope.

1576 James Burbage builds the first professional theatre in London.

1577 Francis Drake begins his round-the-world voyage on the *Golden Hind*.

1585 England and Spain are at war until 1604. Sir Francis Drake sets sail for the West Indies.

1587 Elizabeth I has Mary Queen of Scots executed at Fotheringay Castle.

1588 The Spanish Armada is defeated by the English Navy.

1591 About this time, William Shakespeare starts work on his first plays, *King Henry VI* (parts I–III).

1603 Elizabeth I dies. She is succeeded by King James VI of Scotland, the son of Mary Queen of Scots, who becomes King James I of England.

Glossary

apprentice A person who learns a trade by being employed in it for an agreed period of time at a low wage.

backgammon A very old board game for two players, with pieces that are moved according to the roll of the dice.

ballad A song that tells a story.

barbarian A person from a wild and uncivilized tribe that lived long ago.

Catholics People who believe that the Pope in Rome is the head of their religion.

clergymen Ministers of the Christian religion.

colony A country that has been settled in by people from another country and is governed by that country.

court The place where kings and queens entertain visitors and meet advisers.

dysentery A disease that causes severe diarrhoea and sometimes death.

faeces Waste from people's bodies.

flogging Beating with a stick or whip.

game Wild animals and birds that are hunted for sport and for food.

grammar schools Schools that were originally founded in the sixteenth century to teach Latin grammar. Most grammar schools have been converted into comprehensive schools.

hung, drawn and quartered A punishment that involved hanging a person, cutting them down before they died, removing their bowels and cutting their body into quarters.

jousting A contest between two knights, riding horses and carrying lances.

livestock Farm animals such as cows, sheep, horses and pigs.

Mass A religious ceremony performed by Catholics.

merchant Somebody who sells goods for a profit. Often they trade with other countries.

migrated Moved from one place to live in another.

milliner Somebody who designs and makes hats for a living.

noblemen Men who belong to the aristocracy, the highest class in society.

peasant A person of low social status or class.

pike A weapon with a pointed steel or iron head on a long, wooden pole.

pillory A wooden framework with holes for the head and hands, used to hold criminals as the public made fun of them.

plague A deadly disease which is spread quickly over a large area. It usually refers to the bubonic plague, which was common in Tudor times.

poaching Hunting and catching animals and fish illegally on somebody else's land.

Protestants People who believe that the king or queen is the head of the Church of England.

Puritans Strict English Protestants who first formed their own group in the sixteenth century.

veal Meat from a calf.

venison Meat from deer.

Activities

pp4–5 Who Were the Tudors?

- Use the Internet or books about the Tudors to find a family tree for the Tudor kings and queens. Make a family tree poster, and decorate it with drawings of the kings and queens.

- Imagine you are a Tudor baron. Write a diary, describing the day you have had drinking, eating and playing games.

pp6–7 Riches for the Rich

- Look at the King, Queen and Jack in a pack of playing cards. They are wearing clothes from the Tudor period. Design your own picture cards from another period of history, for example the Roman times.

- Design and write a menu for a Tudor banquet with ten courses. Use the foods described in this book, and any others you can find in books on the Tudors or on the Internet.

pp8–9 Rags for the Poor

- Look in books for paintings from Tudor times. Do you think they show how hard life was for the poor? Think about whether the painters were rich or poor, and how this might have affected the pictures they painted.

- Make a poster showing the 'Great Chain', with God at the top, animals at the bottom and people in between.

pp10–11 Hygiene and Disease

- Imagine you are a newspaper reporter and there has just been an outbreak of cholera in your local town. Write a report about the outbreak, and about how the shocking state of Tudor towns may have caused it.

- Draw a plan of a Tudor town, showing the houses, streets and open sewers. Include rivers and wells where people collected water and washed.

pp12–13 Making a Living

- Write an advertisement for a job in Tudor times. Include the skills required, the benefits of the job, the hours of work and the salary.

- Find out if there are any Tudor buildings in your area. Look at how the buildings were made. Find out about the materials that the Tudors used to make their buildings.

pp14–15 Women's Work

- Make a timetable for a single day in the life of a Tudor cook working in a big manor house. Write down the different tasks for different times of day.

- Write a shopping list to take to a Tudor marketplace. Remember to include a list of items you might be able to sell, as well as items you need to buy.

pp16–17 A Tudor Childhood

- Write a play about a child caught laughing in a Tudor classroom. Assign roles to members of your class and act it out. Think of a suitable punishment for the time.

- Use the library or the Internet to find instructions for the game blind man's buff. Make up a similar game and write your own instructions.

pp18–19 All the King's Soldiers

- Use the Internet to find out about Tudor castles. Now design your own castle. Include a moat, a gatehouse and turrets.

- Write a newspaper report about the English Navy defeating the Spanish Armada.

pp20–21 Religious Tension
- Imagine you are living during the reign of King Henry VIII. Write a letter to your local newspaper complaining about the religious situation. If you are a Catholic, remember to make your letter anonymous!
- Write a short play about a Catholic family being discovered by the queen's soldiers holding a secret ceremony. Assign roles for the priest, the family and the soldiers.

pp22–23 Explorers
- Write an imaginary ship log or diary for the captain of a Tudor ship exploring the Americas or West Indies.
- Imagine you are a sailor on board a Tudor ship. You would have faced storms at sea, eaten dreadful food and probably suffered

from terrible diseases. Write a letter home to your family describing your adventures.

pp24–25 Entertainment
- Use the Internet to find the lyrics of the song 'Greensleeves'. Now try writing your own simple Tudor love song. Choose instruments used in Tudor times to play the music.
- Design a poster advertising a Morris-dancing troupe who are coming to perform in a village square.

pp26–27 In the Tavern
- Write an advertisement for a tavern in Tudor times. What attractions might be described?
- Imagine you are a Puritan in Tudor times. Write an angry letter to your local newspaper complaining about taverns and ale houses.

Finding Out More

Books to Read
Heritage: The Tudors in Britain by Robert Hull (Hodder Wayland, 2000)

On the Trail of the Tudors in Britain by Richard Wood (Watts, 2000)

The History Detective Investigates: Tudor Home; Tudor Theatre by Alan Childs; *Tudor Medicine* by Richard Tames; *Tudor War* by Peter Hepplewhite (Hodder Wayland, 2002)

The Illustrated World of the Tudors by Peter Chrisp (Hodder Wayland, 2001)

What They Don't Tell You About the Tudors by Bob Fowke (Hodder Children's Books, 2001)

Places to Visit
Hampton Court, East Molesey, Surrey KT8 9AU
Visit the state apartments of Henry VIII, see a Tudor kitchen and explore the gardens and maze.

Mary Rose Museum Ship, Portsmouth Historic Dockyard, College Road, HM Naval Base, Portsmouth PO1 3LX
Visit this museum and see the only sixteenth-century warship on display in the world.

St Mawes Castle, Cornwall; Stokesay Castle, Shropshire; and Dartmouth Castle, Devon, were all used for some of the photographs in this book.

Index